Other Books by Lindy Hough

Changing Woman
Psyche

The Sun in Cancer
Lindy Hough

NORTH ATLANTIC BOOKS

The Sun in Cancer

ISBN 0-913028-34-7

Acknowledgement is made to *Truck* and *Io* where some of these
poems appeared originally.

This project is assisted by grants from the National Endowment for
the Arts in Washington, D.C., a Federal Agency, and the Ver-
mont Council on the Arts, the state arts agency in Montpelier,
Vermont.

Photograph and calligraphy: Betty Sheedy

The text was set in Aldine Roman, an adaptation of the typeface
designed by Aldus Manutius in the 15th Century. Composed on
the IBM Composer by Typographics, Plainfield, Vermont.

North Atlantic Books
Route 2, Box 135
Plainfield, Vermont 05667

Principal Distributor:
Book People
2940 Seventh Street
Berkeley, California 94710

For the memory of my father,

Henry Wade Hough (1906 - 1974)

Contents

I   STARTING THE SEEDS

come on in
the night air is
surprising mild

the cats are driving themselves crazy
with their delimited
small spaces

       do you think
       there will be time to talk
       will we even do that
       gracefully or with orange candor
       underneath the snowwhite weight
       of all we have laid on each other
       to be?

Little wise fetus
do you know so much
do you see spaces   colors
          pinks   shapes we've left out
or not fitted into our gestalts

          the spaces are soon filled up
          with directive information

I half don't want you to emerge
& begin the process of losing
one by one, all you see inside
in order to get milk, warmth

          blocking out all these
          vast networks you've known of
          simply because here,
          they don't summon from me
          what you now
                    need

Churchbells proclaim their message of
urgency & timing but briefly, as if to say,
not too long, we realize these are only relevant
to a few, & I think of those who attend,
gracing a house where —
does God dwell there?

     Is that conjunction of bodies
in connection with one another, His & theirs,
made manifest there, any more than
here? At desk,
lamp, fire, hot coffee, child playing?

His presence always among us.
In our yellow sheaves, in
the rich soil, in our turmoil, in
our leavings

They who gather do to affirm
their village identity & yet flickers pass,
their individual fixed eyes strain to catch
the nuances missing all the other days as they
watch the Cross, offer concentration separate
from relation.

> "the world takes its form
>   as a consensus
>   of all the inhabitants'
>   image of their needs . . & capacities"

String Sculpture of Barbara Hepworth

My concerns are round,
          abstract as the hole
puncturing space as through
          a capsule, spewing seeds from dried pod,
opening into
          wave, spiral, a tension of
vortices against which
          open space, the light we see,
is strung, defining more clearly
          enclosed energy and the shadows we work
within.

          As though I were to set up
multiple strings arching their proud backs
          at different lengths
from your involvement
          with space
on a grid of time
          to mine.
As though we would be able to record
          by these non-violent measures
the violence we did to one another
          & the grace we allowed to flower,
O so quietly,
          the sun moving across
the sky with the same quietness   the strings
          hold their position, in analogous vastness.

This would be better than a camera,
          my first thought to record this dance,
because we *make* the strings.
          Like the sun, the strings don't record,
as much as they are part of
          the progressive thought and action.
They direct our attention
          like white swans,
they focus our inaction on action.
But how we did drift from these white
          markings, drifting in a down of details
smothering our faces, how the details
          consumed us and humans do
get themselves down
          absolutely measured down
as though light were capable of
          no response, no discrimination,
simply of being captured in pigeon-hole boxes —
The subtle petty gunfire violence
          we do to our lives,
losing our hearts,
          spacing our heads into imprecise corners.

                              a prayer

Let us at least be
    free as the light coming before us,
open as the spaces stand before we enter.
    Let us have the agility
to become with good grace

these,
let us, if responsibility is
        the ability to respond
never indicate the Other
        is a passel of burdens,
reduce a human to the tiny boxes
        this civilized world packages everything in.
Let us squirm to free each other
        from those boxes and our selves,
when we quarter our own spaces.

Let us not box goldenrod,
        asparagus ferns,
the wind through the grasses;
        wind   space   time, let them
blow us up and out,
        up and free as we came to be when
first-born

        And let the line then, and this love
be light
        as string, but let
the strings in their making
        not tie us tautly,
for surely we are more than our measurement.
        Surely we are more than our strings,
than our castings.
        And if we waver, if sometimes we seem
to be no more than
        the dance we make,
let us remember

a white light and a blank space,
that it was the beauty of simply those
which made us want to speak.

The Second Pregnancy

— How are you today?
— I'm o.k.

>   except that my spine is breaking out in spots
>   the snow that blanketed everything is now filling up
>   the cavities left in my stomach.
>   the suicide on the windowledge is jumping
>   because she has heard a man from below
>   who called up,
>   "Jump! No one gives a damn!"

* * *

If I walked out into the clear white cold air there would be nothing-
ness. Or a whole world of activity between the sewers and my feet:
animals burrowed in tunnels, trees covered with snow until it sinks
into warmer earth, brook running where it isn't frozen, animals
scavenging for food, bearing the cold well because they have sturdy
coats and yet holding their minds tight until some warmer energy
comes, to free them from this frozen world.

It is no longer possible to write about desire or frigidity or orgasm because the mind is so tangled in the body's metabolism, so directed and subhumed by it, that the body is literally a feudal master over the mind. But their interplay is subtle and tenacious: they pull on the rope, each making their weight felt, the nine months pregnant body so insistent of its every condition, the mind so rebellious about controlling its land, its territory, its hopes and desires for the future. So the mind lances on ahead like an outlaw in the new countryside sprung from a feudal barony where the master was impossible, and wages war on all the peasants he comes in contact with. On the loose, he would make a semblance of order but only has the distraught hay-strewn countryside to work with. His relations with everyone are thus discontinuous and outrageous in their obliquity.

Dream of the Collective

Important not to feel deluded, degraded
delighted, denuded or derided. Conspiracies
awaken. In the chest of drawers
is a snake rushing from hospital
to hospital, showing all the fangs
the family has. Somehow I was to
have the baby in a hospital in New York
I wasn't sure which one, was it Fifth
Avenue Flower, or Beth Israel, my
mother-in-law was embarrassed I asked
my father-in-law, my parents and doctors
were no where to be found,
& there was a hurry because I was in
transitional labor and subsequently on a plane,
in a taxi, in a traffic jam. There were
too many people in the streets and no way to
get around the individualism
sticking from each's body
like a radial pointed star's aura.

The mind
peculiar piece of living tissue
that it is, heads on into obscurity
dragging a piece of rope.
It sits down on the rope and begins
to chew it, valuing the children asleep
the tired back relaxing for a moment
which means the breasts too
relax
and begin to drip milk

The mind has learned a
great deal of information. All of it
is null/void
in the face of extreme exhaustion.
No one speaks
No one dares raise a hair's breath
        against the quiet of the afternoon,
        the sun shining on the insistent red-winged blackbirds
        who rise in a flurry to the tree,
        descend again in a vale
        all at once, forty black bodies, to
        the seeds on the snow.

A mind filled
with information.
Past history: past families, past people,
past places.
Past experiences collecting into nothing more
than the gestalt of present action,
blackbirds on the snow like atoms,
on-going.

There is no minute
we are not in the present.
There is no way to live
other than in the present.

The continual drip
of the icicles
confirms this moment's
hold on time,
all else in the mind
unnecessary that does not
force to this realization.

There are no pussy-willows
near by
to bring inside.
Don't
they grow here?
Or is it that I have not looked.

One now, a lean male one
has lost
a sense of the world,
is institutionalized.
He doesn't any longer want to get out.
I am like that about the house.
I must be afraid of the world.
I must be afraid I will eat the world
or the world will eat me.

There are walls
but people say the walls are spongey.
You can walk through them,
move through them like a monkey letting
breezes move through his trees, if you even try.
I am so afraid of the consequences
that I don't try
but I watch the world going on outside
and wonder,
where is it and why am I not in the world.

Most of the old people around me
are also prisoners in their houses,
of their own choice.
But I'm only thirty, and they are seventy.

Presumably they did a lot of things once.
Perhaps they went out to see their children,
just newly married, set up on their own farm.
Perhaps they had a farm themselves
in their day (this is not their day, they say)
rather than a house in the village
and they went to their cows
and their cows came to them.

It is all a matter of degree,
I know that.
I would like to try to walk through the walls.
I wonder if they really are
soft and malleable
or hard, as I usually think of them.
I wonder if they will scrape my skin as
I pass through, or if it will be a smooth passage,
like Death's mirror pulling Orpheus.

Last night a student came over
from the world
His mind was falling apart.
He called my husband a shit over and over
and sat in the livingroom cursing at him,
talking in great abstractions at break-neck pace
about the Kabbalah, superimposing on Richard
the face of the father he hates, who is
flying now to the hospital to see him.
Schizophrenia. The mind starts replicating
cells which can't fit into the existing system,

which ravage and plow under the patterns of hate
and hostility until they bubble up
like an autumn fountain in Venice.

I don't know where it puts us,
any of us in our larger or smaller worlds.
Molly Miranda lies on the floor,
her five-months-old toes in her mouth,
smiling and laughing because she's not
hungry or wet or sleepy.
The infinite sadness of all sentient beings.

Again. Indoors.
Again this enormous
Commitment
To very probable failure,
As though the will wanted to
Involute again, to see the skin
It had forgotten the stripes of.

But angels
Don't decide
Do they have the time,
Energy,
Will,
To guard our sheep this year
To speak through our mouths,
To try our troubled minds
With their composites

The seeds push finally up through
My Mind
On a blowy April peeking-through-soil
Cold day,
Hardly together do we have
Ourselves.

But we don't know how
To stop the show,
And we're glad of that.
We have the blessed
Ignorance
To shuffle on meanderingly
But forward, our arms swinging
and singing,
There, and back again.

The Hermaphrodite

Count Yesseldorf
comes in.

He doesn't know his throat
from his tailpipe.
He carries on an aimiable
conversation as he quietly
becomes high, sitting on his scotch
on the rocks he surveys
with sophomoric pride the people
in this yellow plastic room,
the plastic Parsons' table,
the decorator surroundings the
decorators have created, perched on yellow plastic bar stools
and yellow woven couches.

Out the window on the back patio
is assembled some Art:
huge stage flats, wires, speakers.
It is meant for people to discuss,
why is it art? Another generation
discusses it, and the one who made it
goes to work, seeding the lawns with
rolled up already-grown turf.

Our empathy is with
Count Yesseldorf.
He reads bits and pieces of the Nixon tapes,
he floats in an understanding of the world
and its political necessities,
he waits until the finish.

He lets the baby cry a bit,
he is rocked in the
everlasting understanding of no sex,
of the giant evergreens, taller
than the third floor of the house.

Count Yesseldorf
is nearing an understanding
that it is no longer an option
whether to take his clothes off
before the sun, his Queen;
Count Yesseldorf watches the far-off barn
across the quietude of brown hills
and knows very much
with a firm rock certainity
where his horse, the blue roan,
is grazing.

A Meeting: It is Not What One Expected

Masha: " . . . Send your books, be sure to
write in them. Only don't put "esteemed
lady," but simply this: "To Marya, who
not remembering her origin, does not know
why she is living in this world." Goodbye.

Chekhov, *The Sea Gull*

All day
I had been looking forward
to his coming
like the rays of the sun
on a blowy March day going in and out,
happy moods glancing off one
like the glint of sun from the roofs
bounced from the traveling clouds
chasing the sun

Had telephoned him
in the morning hoping to blend
my need to his in the cold grey Industrial morning
or summoning him
(a colder view)
like Venus summons the lake mists,
gathers them around her to keep
her warm, keep the salt spray

from glancing cross her brow,
tendrils of hair flying across the waves

& when he finally came
I woke bolt upright
stumbled downstairs to be there
be presence to his summoned presence
And yet it clattered away,
a wagon led by a tumbled-down horse
I couldn't get hold of,
conversations that fluted & leapt around the room
not focusing with any real energy on anyone,
a dinner where there were so many
children, villagers, pasts & futures
represented, his eyes were a jangle

There was no way to talk

The conversations I look for with him
I only carry on well with myself
So busy must we both be
trying to place ourselves correctly
in the village,
in our pasts and presents,
in the doings we imagine each other doing

Would you like to go to Israel?
New York?
Australia?
O, New Zealand, of course.
Denver? No, England.
Montreal is closest.

All these places stir like shades
in my mind, speaking a language
we could learn, grabbing at the image of you
as you pass in my mind with
prayers and advice and always a past history.
You fit with all of them
easily as a strand of hair
once it is combed.

But both my son
and my husband resist combing —
For all I know
                    (men are so knotty,
                         better to stick to my own wares
you would too,
every step of the way

That's why my picture of you
is always a story,
continually fueled
by the discrepancies the real you

throws up in the face of
the sand-man figure I make of you

II GARDEN TACTICS

Something is sapping the life of that plant. I touch the leaves, they are limpid as an unerect penis, they are too thin, there is no hardiness and they seem to say, ok, we'll give up. I run my finger over the soil, hoping to see tiny bugs take flight; a clue, dust clouds arise with anger; all I see are some slugs and white aphids, it seems too wet. The plant of the same kind in the window next to it is doing well, blooming; it must be a lack of sun.

The john smells of urine. There are imperfections. How will I ever read all these books, get all this knowledge into my head and streaming back out in the writing, if I have such high anxiety that I can't sit still and read anything but shlock. She who I thought is a lovely storyteller is a regressive lady, going on and on; the stories reveal a jewish story-telling background that has barely been risen above, and these are stories by a novelist I once thought was gold. In the reckoning, one casts the heroes down as strongly and force-fully as the enemies. Who shall remain untouched?

Only he who I rail out in parts of my mind as oppressor, and yet so admire artistically that I can't think of anything better than being able to make gold like his gold. Spin webs like his webs, that each day, even when I sweep them down, are carefully built up again in perfect radial symmetry in corners where people must walk and stoop, or else feel their head for webs moments after running into them.

Or I so admire him that his presence is a thorn, or can we learn to live peacefully and make a world that is not based on subjectivity, but in which we are people, with deep resources and gifts and the leisure and happiness to explore them. The amazement is that we're already doing this; I sort and sort and so does he, we comb the wool from the sun's lambs, and these are

29

tasks that prepare us well for the really hard tasks of loving one another. When we get up from making love or working there is the house in its detail, the garden with its paper bags sopped but still intact, guarding tomato plants I am rooting for in this rain.

In the past week there has been one electrical storm and one earthquake. I was the one of the three of us who felt the earthquake; all of us sitting in Robin's room on the red rug. He looked at my face and it was horror, someone knocking at the door, he thought by my face, but I had felt the floor tip, it was no longer flat and parallel, the earth had heaved. Possible explanations I talked of as we went to check the furnace, me carrying Robin and he again as during the electrical storms incredible lightning flashes feeling my terror through me, flowing out freely as current from me to him, no help for it; it is, I said, either me hallucinating, or a sonic boom, or least likely because we don't live in the right part of the country, an earthquake. But that night we listened to the news and it was the latter: another had been in 1962, another in 1935.

And so we are connected with history, beginning to be connected to the major events in this town and state. For the first time we had everything in common with all the people in this town; there was no difference and the lusciousness of the common experience, though I talked of it with few people, was fine.

But it left, and one is alone again with what can be worked, and if anything can, to prevent disaster and decay, to make it meaningful to live now in this place, in this time. Since we do.

Oh, said Sister Carminita. Focus on chance, light, movement. They will together make a music, make a waterfall, make sparrows tumbling down the rays of sunlight. Make glee. Or, a high degree of happiness.

In America, or this house, or this compartment of my brain, you have to watch words like happy, sad, glee, sadness, response. The social moves inward like a giant wooly bear. It is friendly but then again what do you say to it, how to address its massive *warmth*.

All my life I have had that problem, I sighed to Sister Carminita.

Sister Carminita was clearly everything I wanted to be. A vapor, a sylph, perfect shoes and feet in the midst of *Les Sylphides*. She had no mental blocks, dealt with the white blinding light rather well, found an inward correlative for those faces quiet and expectant looking up at her. She was all I had left behind, all I did not keep running into in the street outside my house, all I had inside of me if only I remembered to look behind the dark green curtains. Invoking the parts of her by washing my windows. Useless to try and find her in the outside world, though the lights and shadings that rang up and down her face often appeared to be mixed with other essences that every seven years or so showed up in the countenance of certain men. O raw illusion. Gradually I had learned, with the tenaciousness of well-rooted cornstalks and the determination of moulding wood, that men represented simple fucking to me with a little insight thrown in like cinnamon on my oatmeal. The insight was often totally wrong, though usually frightfully appealing coming as it did from the "world of men," that dominant land of oz that happened to control the world.

31

O too much, said Sister Carminita. How lovely that you value the sparrows under my arms at last. How lovely that you have allowed yourself the space to *think*, much less perform useful action. O how lovely.

It was lovely. It was the beach in Cape Elizabeth when we walked there together, the three of us, Robin so small. It was the light purple scarf of memory and creatures bubbling in the newly-wet sand.

We have been happy other places. We will be happy here, there will be sunlight and breakfasts that we have together, the tiny birds will come.

If you wanted to move very much today, you would have to ask the air currents' permission, they are pushing down with such an inviolable pressure. The rooms which fall into the setting sun, slipping slowly behind the mountains that ring the town, are actually hotter. Stay in the dining room, the living room. Live in the living-room, which is dark and cool. Moments ago I tried to take a nap in this spangled afternoon which is letting me slip away, giving in to my stomach which was reeling in a bloated toadstool fashion perhaps from a bacterial infection caused by the town's polluted and insufficient water supply, and still felt like an over-full stream, thrusting itself with crashing force down-hill. I lay on my side as one does when one is pregnant, one leg across to balance the weight, but all that was hanging over on the bed was my bloated stomach, which can't be bloated because its only at the most a month pregnant, without a bacterial dance going on inside it.

In this town we are not friendly enough with the villagers to ask about the water supply without implying criticism of *their* water. Even though we have bought a house and lived in it for almost a year now. & you must take the newspaper to know if the supply is polluted; we take the big city paper which doesn't concern itself with the village's water. Let those bacteria dance their natural dance. But maybe, we figure, you can harden your stomach to it, as in Mexico. Or I think that, not him.

You can't fight city hall. Or the day's events. I'm so lax I don't even start what I want to finish. O to be finished already with all these things, and doing something that *really* holds my interest. What would that be, says the tone that asks Robin what he wants to drink after he has said, I want something to drink.

There was a large question about the cats and chicken bones

in the household. The question raged through the house like a fire everytime chicken was served by one of the cooks, and then was forgotten and unsolved in between. One sector of opinion thought that surely the dry bones would arch and catch in the upper pink roof of the cat's mouth, a human finger wouldn't be near to twang it out, and the cat would be in agony for minutes as the bone jabbed further into its mouth. This sector left the bones in a white plastic cup until the other climate of opinion grew tired of seeing them, their smell mingling with the fruitflies from the vegetable garbage, and threw them out on the grass, where the three cats came running to gobble them up. This latter sector thought that whatever would happen would, that it was a good way to dispose of chicken bones without attracting dogs to the compost, and that if it killed off the cats they were too many in number anyway.

Mr. Tarn Comes Fresh From
Mt. Desert

Oh   I have no idea   no not the least which it
would be better to do, or to try to do, or to aim at, this green tree
or this standard over here standing by the house, but something
has to be tried.

Once drove up a man in his stationwagon, and we
painted for him while we were here our life, in all the colors we
knew how, the greens merging into the yellows and flowing down
into the washes of bright red, and the whole hung on the wall and
if we were lucky enough he was charmed, and us also by him, and
if he could not encompass it he said, that's neurotic and not nor-
mal, that hanging on the wall, and then when and where were we.

Our colors overlapped and we talked together too
much, spilling paint on each other, get out of my way! But he left
and we found our own rhythms and tracks again and were all right,
saved as usual by the smallest tendrils, from falling into the water-
fall headlong. We tried to order things coherently from hour to
hour.

But this man had come from the sea, a further attrac-
tion, a further distraction, and reason why we doubly paid atten-
tion to him — although he came with all these languages and all
these lives and names from different countries so it was dazzling
even to talk to him. Not only the sea but the specific bit of sea-
shore that we had lived on and by, he cared enough to look up a
lobster fisherman there who was the only man we had known
quite well, and thus came trailing intriguing bits of seaweed about
this man and his life now, with him. Do you realize, with all the
other crudities we suffered there, all the moments of untenable
existence, how many new mornings we found from having the

35

vastness of the sea to deal with daily, not that we were on it, but that it stood close by in all its awesome variation, changing each day and pronouncing terms and vocabularies with such a largess that we could never begin to be anything but inspired, integrated, resuscitated by it?

Although each day you do live and you do not think, I am inspired. But it eats into your life there and after leaving the sea you realize that *hills*, diaphanous, cows grazing on them in all their variation, are not the same. Or pretend to be. Now we sink into this dark earth and make the best of it, and wait for what will come.

Scores of people go to the sea. That island we lived on has a national park on it, which we never visited. Scores of people go there and camp, never knowing that the yellow canaries are just small warblers, and they have their own experiences there over the weekend that they remember. That happened there, they think, back in the place they live once again. But we *lived* there, and perhaps we shall again; we drove around the island, skirting the national park, never going in it and entertaining a sense of the island that tried to pretend, with a childish superiority, a rebellious righteousness, that it wasn't there.

It's very easy to totally lose one's head. Get up, go through the day, even though it is in one's own house, not standing at an assembly line, and be worn to a nubbin by 10 o'clock, the head having folded in on the body which is so strong with anxiety that it churns the head up as easily as a balloon is pulled under by the swift churning waves at

The phone rings in the middle of the night. We are deep in sleep, a thousand tunnels away at the end of our own fantasies.

"If you don't get your dog Zebaka out of here I'll kill it," says a garble at the other end, raging. Violence, and not awake, not able to understand any of the connections between this message and ourselves, I cry, start crying, the morning folds in on itself as I describe who the owner is, outrage that Mel should have put our name and address on his dog's collar because he doesn't have an address, and lives now at the college where dogs are not tolerated. Outrage that Mel is nowhere to be found, as we try to call him and get him to become responsible for his own animal.

We lie in bed afterwards, try to recover the calm this insanely angry phonecall has caused, make love, Robby later is stormy. But later calm streams out, because I realize that building up the soil (the personal cosmos, the perceptual world) is a gradual proposition, that over time we will add all the material to our soil that will make it rich. I will grow brighter and more perceptive; all the books will be read and understood.

The garden is understood to be (and the passive voice is similar) a proposition involving calm and needing calm also. If I get to what I am saying the perceptions will be there in the total sling of the words. Thousands and thousands of seeds dropped on the earth and only a few take root, germinate, ever become a tree. If I come to the garden jerkily and am harried and harrassed the garden will produce to myself and others only harrassment. I looked out the upstairs window this morning and saw a neighbor's thin strip of a garden, limed freshly. I jumped with anxiety; that is what I should be doing. But I've always jumped like that when I saw another more along a road of progress I thought I wanted to be along; it is the fate of the Psyche daughter with older sisters, older friends, and parents who want the youngest to remain forever young, so they will be able to delay their life processes.

Two months later: the whole push of spring has subsided within me, as summer has plumped out. Things came up in the garden. The soil was rich enough to make everything good. But I'm almost not concerned now: as though some lack of attachment was necessary before I could again see what was happening there. I can work in it, tend its dire needs, but I'm not concerned with whether everything is perfectly in its situation.

How left out the stars are, if my mind can't let them in.

Be diaphanous. Allow light to show through the bubbles in your system.

I am me and we are here but we won't be here for ever.
Forever. We live here now but it's not for always. Which means we
don't have to get used to things we definitely don't like about the
place.

& yet it is beautiful. The stream the hills the varied
topography of the land. There is time now to enjoy it and our life
and write about it if one's expectations of anything aren't too high.
We are more getting our expectations in line with the reality that
sits on its haunches and looks us in the face.

At least there are not deaf and dumb girls handing
me pens with outstretched hands lingering, which have known
constant tapping and little else, every day.

The birds here like each other and get on well. Cats
sit on most of the doorsteps and prowl the back yards. We have
three female cats and just adopted a stray male who is so plied with
food he is defending the territory (3 females and food! what could
be better!) from two other males who just tonight have shown up.

People are only rude if you demand friendship.
They mostly like to be left alone in their localness. Too many
people have moved into this town wanting to be locals. There are
only so many local souls to go around and the real local people are
jealously keeping the ones they have acquired. I used to think I
wanted to be "accepted" but now I have no such illusions. I feel
markedly different and perhaps they are right to keep the covers
pulled up around their eyes till they die, at least. After that we will
inherit the earth for our short time and they can't have any control
over it, so I'll wait. But thank god, we won't be here then.

The sounds that abound here are like the colors
of the assorted kittens. I can't remember or keep track of them in

the smells that overpower. Today I rode my bike down by the river, following it by its curved dirt road, and the smells were glorious. Even though my throat kept manufacturing needless bubbles the smell of the moist green woods on either side of me came like a velvet green moist tongue.

Gradually I'm developing a schema of living through a day without having societal images of all the colors I inhabit follow me around, haranguing depressing speeches from their perches in the cupboards about my behavior, dancing on what fragile notions of a courage I have, eating the leaves off regularly every night and leaving only a jagged stem in the morning to begin the day with. Root canal work. I have put those rotifers to bed once and for all. Almost.

The man read his poetry, although he said he hated poetry readings and never went because they were such a drag, like he was sitting on top of a huge beach ball his legs wouldn't fit around, with no hope of standing on firm ground very soon. He was dying to get through with it and sighed a great deal. He rested his book of poems on a plastic display case of an old shoe which had brown moss on it, and was condensing moisture on the underside of the plastic. He was thus in effect part of the exhibition and obviously cared not very much for it, since he was draped over this otherwise irrelevant work of art in Miss Smiley's exhibition of photographs.

I felt, listening, as though there were a diesel truck permanently passing my own vehicle, that roar going on in my mind even though we were sitting quietly listening to him. I tried to get hold of single words but he had a commitment to beauty that blocked all sense and sensibility out. The other thread that wove all this together was that he was the brother of an estranged wife-husband team who talked loudly at the beginning of the reading: "How is your household? I'm teaching the children to sweep up in my house" as though they hadn't seen each other in months, when the last time was probably yesterday. & so we sat, the other five people other than the immediate family, inside this family web on a beach ball.

The words coalesced into a single mass as hard as ice cubes. We were all imprisoned in that mass, except that the family members had the past history of their relationship, when they had first met each other, what each was like when the couple's children were born, to ruminate on during the reading. The rest of us were *really* frozen. I was out for the fun of it on a Sunday afternoon that was unbearably hot ("Thank you all for coming to this reading on this hot hot day," said the brother) and didn't mind being part of an ice cube for a while because it would melt as soon as I got outside, since it was a *very* hot day.

Which isn't always true. One goes to a meaningless event, on the theory that doing *some*thing is useful, that the world holds so much variety that something will be able to be observed that is helpful, yet the emotional feeling pervading the bloodstream when one comes home from an utterly depressing event, or a wrong-headed event, is not neutral. In other words, what people do *does* matter, does have an effect on the individuals who participate. One is *not* neutral and cannot escape being effected for better or worse. If the expectations are high there is usually disappointment, if the expectations are low and the event is a bomb, there is that wasted time which could have been sailed better.

Probably in five years I will no longer be exposing my sacred person to ice cubes at all. Or I'll be unintelligibly part of a consuming fire which will change me into some thing that no longer needs speech. These tiny developing pea-words in a pod that can itself be eaten.

41

At least I am fairly sure most of my words are eaten by women, and those men who are in a position to be eating the words of a woman like me. I eat, by women, most of the words that come my way. Which implies a certain lack of selectivity, i.e. I do keep coming in a steady flow all of it, and eating the kinds of things I've learned to like best, over and over. But a lot gets in that is sad and depressing and makes me angry, because my toleration for what is growing in the general garden is so high. i.e. If *they* planted it, the identification with what all ladies do during the day carries a certain distance, so I am discovering new people who perceive the general situation of life in this era in a way that shows where the stream was at its heights. Rocks strewn here and there, the land compacted with a wash of sand that is still ringing with the weight and density of such surging brown torrents. I remember that height, and they certainly do, so writing about it I suppose we are thinking of straining for how the road felt when it was being cut away, eroded into in great gashes, as the stream carried whole buckets of its dirt away to put on some other bank, which could hardly have been said to need it.

Let me tell you the extent of the damage. Let me tell you the boundaries of the muddle to which I personally, inch by inch like crawling towards a ravine down which boulders can crash with just a finger-push, have come close to.

There is a stigma. There is a baby crying.

There is hardly any time between feedings, i.e. these first weeks we looked for rainbows in the cold March wind and found none.

We had no idea where we were. Birds came back. Books came back. Ravens kept landing with their impossible sooty wings and strutty stride at the birdfeeder, besting the bluejays and both of them keeping out the smaller finer species, lurching with their cold March dignity towards the seeds, hulls though they were, trying to find enough to eat.

We gave them hardly anything, we villagers. We felt the conservative nature of our own inadequacy and terror, and had nothing to spare. We hoped spring would come because our bones were brittle, the long underwear was grafted to our skin and we couldn't imagine feeling cozy without it.

A woman came from the larger town close by, ostensibly to see the new baby. It is a ritual observed wherin one sees all manner of people one would not have reason to see otherwise. She gave me, as present, a novel I had never heard of, by someone immensely popular now (so the book suggested) but nothing on the cover or the back blurbs was recognizable — as though a whole set of newspapers and magazines and reviewers had manufactured these comments about a book that didn't really exist. It was fat and major-looking, but totally unheard of, and it came no clearer for looking at it than she herself did. Through the murkiness of this

43

state of no sleep, caused by a month-old-baby (February is a leap year, so don't forget to add three days on, she will be a month old on March 18th, therefore, not March 15th) I could see this woman was not happy. All her reasons were external and we combed through them, both of us knowing this was not where the food was: their house was above the town and should be in the town, there was no snow so they hadn't been able to ski, the winter had been dismal. She didn't know anyone yet in the town.

I understood, but I couldn't say anything that would carry the depth of my understanding like a new carpet to her, to put under her feet. She had had images of how it would be: herself in this town, working in politics, herself in the house, managing and happy. The way she felt and looked to herself was . . . a drudge on the point of tears, always, staring into the area above the trees out the window; this had not been her image of herself.

I couldn't suggest a thing that would be right. A women's group, a job, living in the village rather than the slightly larger town. She had reasons why all of these things wouldn't work, although to me they seemed bits and pieces that could put together a life, gradually. I could see none of my suggestions were anything other than hulls to her; she would go on being unhappy and things would always be massively imperfect because she was bedded down with unhappiness. It was the most stimulating thing in her life, a constant soap opera she didn't have to turn on, which while she did the dishes she could listen to, buzzing and humming inside her head with inaudible music and a rousing organ. It plugged into hostility and resentment which were so far from being surfaced (her exterior darling and charming, childlike in its naiveté and simplicity) that they provided always this internal music. To the outside observer nothing was wrong, but this woman was on the brink of lunacy. The calligraphy and music lessons aside, which she had chattered about on the phone (phone conversation topics) were never heard from again. Perhaps it was her husband's fault, the job had consumed so much time and he hated it anyway. She let this drop like a stray powderpuff from her pocket book and it rolled across the floor, untouched, glowing in the sunlight like the hermetic rock it was.

I felt sympathetic and yet when she left I stormed around wanting to break windows, feeling a freak when I went outside and stood in the cold March air and wanting to hug that air, that cold village stillness to me like a warm kitten.

Now we are left with the sun and the potatoes boiling. The baby is asleep. It is a cause for rejoicing. I am not asleep: past that, past all the reckoning of what to do, there is nothing anymore from now on but just to grab time, and run away with it to the Sands Hotel, to the Fountainbleau, to Grossinger's, to the Bahamas. I won't use up my days on such women ever again. And know I will, because they are a part of me, part of me walked out the door and got into the car with her, but my sympathy turns into once-removed empathy, which turns into use: *I use you*, I cry out after her form retreating down the driveway; you can kill me later on after you find out I'm only interested in using you as an object of my scrutiny. My good husband says to me, you're like a man to her. You seem to have it all together, you're almost blasé. She hates you out of her desperation and as she pours out her frustrations she is hating you for not being as desperate as she; by your very lack of desperation you have, with her consent, strung her up in this demeaning and supplicating position.

But it is all she knows. She feels more comfortable there than where I am.

And so there are no more careful forms. There are no more expensive fruits and vegetables; it is all too expensive. Unlike her, we have pared down in order to stay alive, there are no more raspberries; the strawberries were probably killed by the lack of snow as an insulator, there are no more asparagus plants, no more artichoke hearts. Items that I grew up with are too expensive to buy now, so we go visit our parents who can still afford them because they have invested in the stock market. We are marginal members of the society, unlike her; we have definitely left the city, the movies, plays, museums behind. We don't miss them anymore than we miss artichoke hearts. We can live here on chard and spinach and grow our own limited foods and take care of each other's bodies and minds and souls best we can.

i

It does seem to be a disaster
to be a woman in this time. I can't
triumph over the sense of frustration
that fills everything up I do.

I painted a table white
& left it out after
the darkness fell

& it was wet
when I brought it in,
more wet
than when I painted it.
Things like that,
the fuckups of every day
depress me.
They're like the prosiness
which lives in my head now,
inhabits this poem like stuffing,
all sparrows
no purple martins.

Maybe I don't put my house
high enough to catch the better currents.
Maybe the stream's been diverted.

But I'm lost now,
wandering in the woods for berries,
barricaded in an old house on the other side of
a door I can't keep closed, from
long hairy arms trying to get at me,
wondering how any woman
makes of her life
more than an elaborate minute-to-minute holding company,
more than a sham.

It's exhausting,
trying so hard every day, all day
to coordinate life
and accomodate it
to my proportions.
Others fuck around, screw each other,
live in the now and bask in their counterphobia.

I can't do anything like this.
My size is changing now,
I'm not comfortable.
Some days I seem to be pregnant and some days not,
how I look is everything now, a real attempt to *be*
a sexual object, since all the men I know are

taken anyway, with that. We all grew up in the same
era.

But there's no man
who's going to save me.
I don't have any sense of a sequined self
which will beckon
"the man I love"

One's alone with minimal conditions
with all the prehensile organization
which co-ordinates the rest of the world,
a web among webs

I don't give a shit
about any man or any salvation
based on balling one man

& no family or friend relationship
is going to save me.
I'm alone
as any cow sitting under the trees
waiting patiently for what's next,
the brown blob
of her thoughts
looking out of blinking
fly-irritated eyes.

I don't know what will come.
I wait, abhoring the passive,
and societal actions seem to arrange themselves
around me. He seems to be following me.
My mind is following him, keeping too much track,
not laying my own track before me as I go.
I follow him because I'm bored with myself,
can keep more of a handle on my life when I am stimulating
to my very self. We move swiftly & one concern runs out
before we have supplied the other, we don't know the speeds
we are running at now until it is pain-stakingly clear.
I would like to be able to manage my life,
which means, not be led in circles by my thinking.

Yet always open
to the suggestive act,
the world loaded with
Christ & Buddha & your form
everywhere I look.
My back is itchy & when people write from England
that it's good at least one marriage seems intact
I jump, startled, & think,
the whole continent, the whole fucking continent
is afloat, and we are swimming fast to try
& grab hold of it.

You must not be afraid.
You must go at your fear
at a run, hands up,
like the wave meets
the eye of the storm

If you are afraid in day
you must travel by day,
meeting the bandit sun
and tussling with his robber sunbeams
they will want to rob you
of all the strength you have.

The planets, disinterested and
dependent on the sun,
will not help you.
In the end you'll die like cinquefoil
and in the whole set of the species
it won't have come to much,
a good life,
a good death,
rain in a cycle of rain

Your friends
will be seen simply
as others of the same species
interested mainly
in their wants, desires, needs
and if you talk in a way they can understand
you will lose the voice that speaks
softly, wordlessly,
to others who are outside the system
and outside the world.

The Sun in Cancer

My work and my garden grow.

I think I will
abstract myself
from every man, and
tend to small things:

chipmunk, line of swan, crest of
yellow warbler.

In this way the connectives
will be left out
to all but me,
and tunnel
I will deep down
where it is safe,
like other women crawl into bed
alone, reading until they put the
light out,
the night outside smelling so good,
so fragrant, so full of new spring —

Are there other places I can live
where there will not be a question
after every tiny sprig planted,

where the baked powdery bones
of my father that ran through my fingers
will not be irrelevant?

I'll have to let more people in.

Perfection in situations is not
to be strived at but rather
a livability,
a lack of stress that makes
four people happy, not just myself.

Dandelions in high grass blow in the wind,
not remembering my father's indiscretions
and my mother's stoic pride.
Something other than dignity
makes the ferns unfurl.

III   VIRYA: JOYOUS ENERGY

Letter to My Mother From Northwood Campus

"By being touched, moved, and opened by the experiences of the soul, one discovers that what goes on in the soul is not only interesting and acceptable, but that it is attractive, lovable and beautiful."

Hillman, *The Myth of Analysis*

1.

Dear Lady. It is not in how beautiful
our patina is, whether our shoes are shined
whether the nose is runny or the face washed
or whether these people are beautiful or ugly.

People are dropping dead in India now
and Sylvia Porter continues to discuss
how Americans will move up, class by class.
You did too, once;
when you were young
you had the flexibility
not to scuttle your fears
underneath plants, underneath
the new abstract painting,
all the back roads must have been
sunsets to you once, as they are
now for me.

I look over at your wig,
which you don't mind getting wet,
and my jacket needs to go to the cleaners,
and we argue about that.
If I sent everything to the cleaners
you would want me to
I would have no time
to watch my mind
or your mind;
I would have no time to
watch the steam rising,
the bird outside finding his way,
his food as the dead drop in India.

Those dead are not far from
my thoughts, even though our pancakes
taste good. I'm not for a minute
fooled by this luxury, I sit at ease in it
but you've brought it, and
I realize it could be gone tomorrow,
that my cat doesn't have the ease
to enjoy being inside
without his bowels turning to water.
Most of our differences come down
to ease: what we have sacrificed
to find it or dodge it.
Most of what occupies me
you don't find pleasurable,
have left behind with the depression,
and though you are proud
you lived through it
you insulate yourself best you can

from the next one.

The ways of the soul are dark ladies
to me, to find and follow out;
I see them wend in and out of the grey branches,
a foursome of habited nuns who carry with them
a blessed joy in every occurrence of
the natural world. I seek men
who work with stone, who work with wood
and words, but I don't glorify them
any longer. If they stick with me
it is because I have a vision
they are interested in,
they sense someone besides the woman
that is me walks alongside me,
and they cohabit with her as I do.

Women I love
fall alongside the road, dead bodies
a central government, proud and defiant
and deluded as any empire,
refuses to help. These women
join my proud dark ladies and
pull me along, we walk around the ponds here
and their faces are in the trees,
singing softly, October wetness matting their leafy
faces, silent to anyone who is moving so fast.

2.

Dear lady of the nights growing old,
I may have glowered,
a poppy shrinking into a teardrop.
You pronounce me erratic.
Why, you say, do you dangle
from the streetlamps
and yet march in submarine procession
to a rhythm of oppression?
Where is the consistency here?

I answer:
because I am young
I don't yet have bitterness,
If I lose my way
it is because the bats
lost their radar
before I was born.
The crown prince misplaced his jewels,
his fiancée, his map
of the new world. I wait, I say,
for a bus that comes
only when I watch very hard
the fire that licks from Eros'
golden fingernails.
Churchsteeples made of wood
topple into the sacristy at these occasions,
the local people watch with confusion,
but the dead are still lined up along the road.

The dead can't hold their meetings
in the new Knights of Columbus hall.

Sunsets err also.

I can't move any faster
than the heaviest, ugliest lady
at the five-and-ten checkout counter;
my fate is tied to hers
precisely because I revere systems of life
which flow into my fingers and
string her baby around her neck, choking her.

My toes feel the dust from her
warped, hunchbacked body
as it disintegrates and
the rocks heaped over her casket
are ready to heap onto my breasts.
Sometimes they are immovable,
sometimes they are on top of me already
& I can't get them off.

3.

In the history of psychology,
Psyche at one point became mind,
and mind became brain, and head

became equated with soul.
All that leaves out where I spend
my nights of terror, a rationalism
I no longer live with,
a shadowy husband you assume I'm married to,
but who I've left long ago.
I'm set up in different quarters now.
When we talk pigeons
walk into our plates and we eat feathers,
because none of the assumptions are in common.
We speak of daily terrors
but these are not where the soul lives;
these are not the waterfalls
where the soul swims free.

My dark ladies
live in a field where the trees still stand,
the wind still blows through them, apparent
and causing movement,
but my mind now can catch
glimpses of death, of other voices,
of pride and humanity.
When I walk alone it should be
that you can walk easier because
I've taken on some of the awkwardness
you must feel, approaching death,
but I know
each lady must find her own
tussle with death.

I work on mine every day.
I wonder how you will meet yours,
and because it is unspoken or
the words are not there to speak of it,
we smile,
the syrup is poured on the pancakes,
the dead drop by the side of the road
in Indian and America,
the paintings go up on your walls,
and we both know
the charge:

work out your salvation with diligence,
as Buddha said,
and don't be surprised
by anything except the beauty
& ugliness you have not internalized.

i

I want to sing
high-pitched like
a seal in the night
after Delius has gone home,

far far away comes the sound,
ringing in his ears as he
makes his quiet preparations
for bed in his cold flat,
quiet mystical snow sifting
down in the streets of Cracow,
go back, young man
says the voice of the seal,
Delius knowing he can't
go back to England or any of his life
before this minute,
that he's in the propeller of a plane
only pushing itself higher
into the sky, climbing cloud
over cloud,
lifting itself up by catching
the far-rushing wind neatly
underneath its wing-span.

A little boy, far below flying a kite,
thinks of his kite's crossbow fleetingly
as he runs as fast as he can pell-mell
down a rocky hill, catches a glimpse of the
plane above and thinks of its wings:
that they are similar to his kite's width,
but can't see Delius' mind
mashed up in the propeller, dangling body
hanging, bone by bone,
dragging through the vapory sky

A man and a woman talk, sitting in their livingroom,
all they have made around them. In the bookcases,
all their books. In their rooms, the children they
have made. They talk of their life together, trying
by building sentences, by letting the words which flow
out of their mouths like molten aluminium frame up
the meaning of their life together. They talk, trying
to ascertain by putting these sentences together,
what their life together is. The words circle them,
bind them in, they try to corral their life together
endlessly by new words, putting new value on different
situations they have been through. They use so many
words, so many sentences, that the meaning they have
to one another becomes obscured through the many words.
The words seem to take on a life of their own, to
be rationing feeling between them, because they have
made the words more important than the feeling they
have for one another.

In their heart of hearts, they want all of this to
stop. They want to just be in the house, to circulate
around each other being happy, amusing themselves,
and call that the life, but they have gotten stuck
in sentences and sentences of syntax, and finally the
words confuse and confound them utterly. They are not
able to use words well at all anymore, they utter them
with finality, hurl large hurtful sentences and then
immediately regret them. They lose the meaning of words,
which is dangerous since they are writers and words

are to have primary value in their lives. They know that
words are, for each of them separately, a large part of
what sustains each, and that were they to start a new
life separately, they would begin it in large part by
using the same words, simply in different livingrooms.

Realizing this, they stop.
They stop talking.
They hit on the idea of only showing love through physical movement,
through non-verbal means. They make love: a deep pervasive
warmth flows out from the seven centers of their bodies. They
flood each other with warmth. The man later does marvelous things
for the woman in the house, the woman is kind and gentle
and soft in her actions about the house, trying wordlessly
to make it comfy and cozy for the man. They save themselves
by starting over and making believe that they know no words
except of calm, slow feeling and that those very words are soundless.

iii

The action of emptying the trash if done correctly.
The action of sifting out what is of use.
The action of determining if anything is of use.
The action of taking first one very small step,
letting go, of taking another, of seeing if that works,
of sitting down if it doesn't work.
The action of walking, once one can take a few steps.
The action of believing one can walk
only comes after one has shown oneself
that step follows step.
Feet go one/right/after/another.

Robby learned to skip today.
He skips everywhere now.
To find the clues, he skips.
He first did it two hops on a foot at a time,
then when I did it for him, he watched very carefully,
and did it: one hop on one foot, then on the other
foot. That is skipping.

Miranda is learning to walk
and Robby is learning to skip.
The complication of the one to the other
is exactly the difference of five years.

iv

The name of the game is love,
or power, or
impeccability. Or
integrity. But no one knows
what any of those terms mean,
good taste is variable,
what is good taste to one and
totally necessary is
anathema to another.

I came downstairs and opened the
curtains. There was a certain amount
of good taste there, and respect,
it was an act not of daring but
of common sense. We want just
enough madness to open ourselves
up, but suicide is not an alternative.
Writing is not shimmying up trees.
Writing is not what you think it is.
The internal dialogue just keeps going
on and on, endlessly.

All these leaves have fallen down from our trees
as they do every year and
once a man came with his children saying could
we have any of your leaves for men,
meaning we want to stuff underwear for some
dummies to sit by cornstalks placed high in a teepee
with pumpkins around and

the touchingness of there not being
for free really anywhere leaves take all
you want I said not able to communicate
to his sad face which was the face also of the
lost gas station owner in the movie *Gatsby*
how totally touching he was

not to have even leaves your own to rake

And so I went on wherever I was going when
he came and came back to see a bit fewer leaves
and them gone, to wherever they lived
and dummies made that I'll never see

I wonder why I didn't talk to him
all our New England pride which is just another
way of saying uptight shyness

The quiet face quickens.
The face at the door
malgré all intent,
malgré all human plans
quickens the blood, a rush
to the face.

I react to the work
only after having responded
to the person,
but still I am
not totally a humanist.

Our commitment is to the world
of things: meaning systems,
meaning how animals deck it out,
but not through any other than
the human mind.

No one seems to be able to
figure anything out
without it going through a mind.
If I learn about social systems

or the herring gull's world
it is not so much a love of birds
but of the understanding
that has been able to show
what birds do.

Do you understand about larches:
those brilliant Halloween trees
which are totally unrevealed
until the last minute before the frost,
an eleventh hour tree:

                    Time so precious
so jammed up because of imminent death,
the brilliant larches orange-yellow
before the hard frost hits

This life,
this procession on the periphery,
what was said in
the autumn of the eclipse,
when we foresaw
how to make heat
hotter
when we summoned
rational arts

Moving across the country
to make our family a Republic
breaking taboos
as we came across them
in ourselves

Surely we worry about ourselves
as we worry about the staying power
of the Nation,
sure that we have done ourselves in
and wait for the fall, the crumbling,
but we have marvelous tenacity.

We'll catch the floor
before it rots
Heat the fire
but not burn the floor
to warm our house,
not coming back to ascendancy
by any means other than
the careful quiet dance we do,
lighting each others' eyes

lighting again and again
the happy spark
in your obsidian eyes
as scales melt into scorpions
as silence passes
again into difficulty,
it will begin again.
Everything always begins again,
until it doesn't.

Virya: Joyous Energy

for Kathy at 15

Small.

Think, in order to calm
one's self down,
about separate small acts,
each one important
& done beautifully,

         all building up
         into a world
         one can inhabit.

Things make sense,
         thus.

People do
      what they want:

they create their own
chaos, their own
fences,
muddling themselves as clearly as
were they to take black
& blue paint,
spread blotches
all over their bodies,

string viscous webs
between their torsos
& their arms,
a sticky unmovable mass —

I can only see
one day ahead,
must beware others' schedules
becoming mine,
in the name of co-
operation.

To co-operate so well
so effectively
one can do nothing alone,
is always a bicycle wheel,
never a pair of legs.

So to explain
your mother's absence,
in thought, word or deed
is to say
she is feeling what
she wants to do when dis-
connected to her family's
desires, whims, commands, needs —

how she thinks when
she has the time,
all the time in the world,
to activate what her life is —

And yet she also
will have to learn to put space
between herself and the event

                    the tree against the vast blithe sky
                    defines itself,
                    so green, its leaves only seen
                    well in isolation

She must not place her being
too close
to the event,

lest she become
object on object —

A bit removed.
Light flies in and around
the occasion, a bird
filtering the sunlight
from St. Peter's dome.

Being open,
joyousness flowing
like molecules
among the events
of sentinent beings.

The height of careful pine trees,
trees which watched this hotel grow,
trees which knew the original building,
    its verandah all around the outside of the first floor,
trees which watched
        cars replace buggies and
        change, through the 20's, 30's, 40's, until
        cars look like what Robby cuts out, glossy color
        photos of long shiny luxurious
        apartments riding on 400-million-year old oil;

trees which watched
        babies run where this house now stands,
heard babies cry and
        family arguments rise and fall until
the children, grown, came to regard
        decisions as important and if not binding
        imperative,
came to decide not to be here, not to
        man the hotel,
to identify with other trees —

Trees which I know
        no one has looked carefully at,
trees with deep roots which

when surface, look like stone,
        so tough,
trees older than me
outlasting me,
green shimmering in afternoon sun-fall
which I could never paint,
though I developed a whole skill
        of color awareness and color shading;
trees that will go on being here
            long after I am hundreds of miles away,
            looking out at my own sugar maples,
            thinking how to preserve them,
            strengthen them against the wind & snow
            winter will throw this time in Vermont;

trees which seem so incredibly strong
            so full of integrity
            harming no one, no man
            and yet dependent on man's good will,
which could chop them down in a moment's rash decision
        of "improvements"
Trees I worry about you,
            because many of the plans around here
            seem slipshod and shortsighted and
            destructive

Trees which in my female, motherly, over-developed
            empathy and altruism
I can no more save
        than I can myself.

81

I take the backroads everywhere now because
I want to prove to myself that I am wedded to
Vermont and all its difficulty that I am not
expecting ease or for a minute dependent on ease
and am totally patient with the hardest life
situations even though I am not in the heat of
any moments that would totally undo me except of my own
choosing men and women can do what they want
although they will suffer immeasurably for their vision

When I follow them out and they come out where
they are supposed to it is a victory to me I
even don't mind seeing the young boys dressed
all in red checkers proud of their guns and totally intent
on the kill in the middle October drizzle, I like
seeing the men going to work wedded to the harshness
of whatever their job is, it is pretty difficult I am
one with them in the urgency to not live in a manner

that would indicate there is any ease whatsoever or
that this country has any ease because whatever ease I
have seen has been purchased at such great cost to the
other inhabitants who have been blocked out of the mind
intent on ease, at others' expense and although others
probably say of me she is living an easy life not for

82

one minute does my manner indicate so to any who know me
and that is perhaps the greatest kindness I can offer.

So many times
you blasted,
        from your full egoism,
trod heavily on top of,
what I considered lovely and sacred —

I stopped, always,
              with amazement
and later understood
              I must have sought you out
for that,
        to force me to re-embrace
more tightly
                    what I thought precious,
beautiful, and
                    yes, even
                         sacred.

Robby: I will give you a kiss
            if you give me a bowl of cereal
Lindy: I will give you a bowl of cereal
            if you will let me wash your face
Robby: I will let you wash my face
            if you will read me a Narnia chapter
Lindy: I will read you a Narnia chapter
            if you will get into your jammies
Robby: You can spell those (gesturing to words
            Duchamps, Satie and Cage) with my letters
            on the ice box
            if you will put them back in their alphabet
               when you're done

Lindy: You can exorcize out the spirit in my life
            if I can enjoy the sweet look on your face.

IV NEW MORNING

Little tiny pink flowers all in a row. To plant such
little flowers. To have them coming up, observable.
We will wait till we have a garden. Can't you see how
lovely it will be in spring? Can't you feel the sun, the
freshness the days will tumble onto your face?

We told ourselves all this during the winter.
We thought, mainly we should get smart during the winter.
Sew little patches on the tears in our clothes.
Plant little flowers in our bodies which go
off as rockets, without somehow killing us.

Very quietly the little flowers are blooming.
Very quietly one is learning more and more.
    All is not contained in the social body,
      there are many people, there is a large, grey Mind.

    All the lovely people, where have they all gone now?
    O, it is lonely, it is not lonely, there are kitchens
      around which people talk, there are people,
      but where are they all?

Beautiful
and most beautiful
and then again beautiful.
We are the masters
of the transcontinental railroad.
Spies
        applaud in the night:
peeking out from the
tattered curtains, they
watch our doings.
We say the right things
at the right times.
They circle to get on top
of us, a suitable
position from which
to best us,
and then leave, filing out
into the 30° below night.

We don't say
a word to one another.
We know we partake heavily
of each others' mystery.
Were we to use one another
fully we would
use up our time here,
burn out a survival candle

that must last for years.
We don't want to start
the wreck of the world
the eclipse of the sunrise
and so all our motions
are elaborately under-extended,
a shyness belies our ages,
as it settles us into rigidity, circumspection.

You are so archly silent, so evenly tongue-
tied, as am I.
When I write about you
it's an anthropomorphism
making the night, the stars, the cold
            the bone cold we're growing fond of,
into a person. It's almost like constantly
writing about myself,
the privatism and egocentrism
that can see no further
than one's own breath.

The river flowing
underneath the ice
combats this.

Creating another life
might combat this,
if it was handled skillfully.

Being more privy to the spies
of knowledge
than emotion
might combat this.

It is symptomatic of
a human relational problem,
of what is sexuality,
what is the boundary of friendship, of the
nuclear family,
that I still involve myself
with the question of you.
I want
      marriage with everyone,
        a family bigger than two parents and two children,
        no affairs, deep friendship.
        I refuse to accept the world's definition of
        what means most to me, in any way.
        But you're the main person
        I would people my walls with.
        Or the referrent my mind dreams up
        in its infinite egoism of identification.

A View of the Stone

In the stone is movement
particles changing & dissolving &
creating themselves into new structures
As much as we have to be aware of our words
& hear the other that puts them into our heads,
you have to be aware of that energy speaking to you
from the stone, & fight
not to drown it out in
your own speaking, your own mind's talk

Thus there is no stasis
in the piece you look at
you bring your self and your body's torque
to its grid of play,
& leave refreshed or used up by the contact
it taking your lust into it and making something
better with it than you could have made alone,
dancing in the streets
of your alone-soul

Your mind though exhausted should only become
strong
by learning the stone's tensions & balances
which are so much greater than your's
You and the stone become more beautiful

93

and are more available to others because you have
changed each other: others now besides you can hear
because you are the bridge between the stone's talk
and the world which talks as you do

When you are picking up the stone
& putting it into the truck
or lugging it around
it is speaking not a human speech
but continually moving inside itself
in the same way I am moving within myself
while we are talking nonsense to each other
in a totally suggestive way
But we hide behind our talk & it keeps us from action.
The contact with the stone is cleaner because it
doesn't admit of such discretion.

None of these meetings are impossibilities
but we have to listen carefully
to be capable of the correct responses
not jump the gun & shoot the stone or each other
or drown out the silent-speech
in our miasma of words

This, like everything else that seems concerned
with the core of our lives is,
sadly if we are lacking it,
a matter of belief

It's hard for me to be patient
and wait my time.
I feel leaves curling red into my hand,
caterpillars changing from furry to velvet
within my palm.
That is a stimulation we used to play
into each others' palm with our fingers,
lightly grazing the inside of your excitement
like a bare toe flirting underneath a table
with an unaware leg.
We still have such ticklishnesses
in different ways;
we are more sophisticated, we catch ourselves now
before we fall over the cliff, & are relieved.

I am saved existential despair because I watch
the world. It gently changes. It is changing all the time,
if only I look, I can see it. Whenever I have looked,
it has been there to watch, a different child
put there by fairies, as complex
as I allowed myself to see it.

My time will come, the world breathes with bubbles
like a river to the inside of me, who hears,
who does know how to wait, who is a woman

looking out the window at children playing,
glad I'm not chasing a red ball across the street,
glad I'm not fantasizing about a toy,
or the next birthday.
I fantasize about changing.
I dream about being the changeling the world is.

I like my age that waits for arms to reach down
from some luminous place and enfold me.
I like my age that understands the river meeting the ocean,
that becomes the river & slows to the ocean.
It all coheres; the gaps I can't put together now
will be gathered up. I feel about my younger despairs
like the girl speaking of the insane asylum today:
it is necessary to get one's trip together if only
to prevent ever being *here* again.

Each year the body has been more revealed to me.
Each year the plan has appeared more coherent.
Each year I have lost
and found myself just in time.

A morning, like all the others.
The great dogs
range over the hill.
A thump on the porch and they
are here, eating the cat's food.
They are large and immoral, trampling over
all we have, carrying away
a broken piece of a blue dish they smashed.

I detest the dogs.
In my virulence is all the distaste
I feel for this place, where a cultivated disorderliness
lives in the inhabitants' eyes. People here are cruel,
by their sins of omission. Or perhaps it is that with
so few, one is rammed up, with one's insistent needs,
against the few, who cannot be,
running breathlessly
in their own Purgatories
anything but selfish and cruel.

And is not marriage
a smaller town, where the inhabitants are self-sufficient
screened off from the outside world, saying,
strangers are so cruel —
no matter how imperfect you are, I would rather be

with you, and let the rest of the world go hang —
but one seeks in the eyes, then, of
the other, a restitution, a solution for one's own
soul-sickness. Perhaps what we are learning is that the
town will not do, that the human himself is the only real
polis, not to seek
the cure in another
but in one's own revitalization.

I have known that for years.
But in the haste to build a perfect union,
built a superstructure of dependency.
It is a quiet thought,
     comes while sewing,
but still my actions, the desperation
     of my energies, come out of the old model,
do not accord.

"And this our life exempt from public haunt,
  finds tongues in trees, books in the running brooks,
Sermons in stones, and good in every thing.
I would not change it."

           Shakespeare, *As You Like It*

Let us observe:

      the poet stutters
      for strength.

      If he be a man,
      such stuttering,
      in the face of a world which moves
      with precision over charts,
      graphs & systems
      is painful.

      He stutters for strength.

      He must not look
      to the practical world,

99

the feminist movement,
the household,
the energy crisis,
Washington & data banks
                    for strength.

So doing,
all his indirectness
will seem to be imprecise.
He will demand more and more
clarity,
and phase himself out of his own sight.

If he look too directly
at all his eyes fall upon —
stones, trees, oceans
in trying to save them
he will no longer hear them speak,
his solutions will dominate his mind
until he is thinking of thorazine
and pumping it through his body
in any number of forms, dulling
dulling

He will become hopelessly discouraged
squaring off his life
in a series of probable hustles,
his need to solve the problems

that will bring us all down
uniformly,
like all sides of a raft
combining with his need for money
and power
to create a tight grill
as badly organized as
a bad pie crust, too stiff
& not holding together;

he will dance
when the soul plays a
wry solipsistic tune
& forget the indirect,
the moment of precision
& ceasing anything but seizing
that moment as occasion;
insight which has informed his
processes like blackness to stars
in the past, and led him on
fruitful searches

will seem sloppy & imprecise

Losing his ability to
prize the obscure,
if he sees himself as standing
revealed in a

revealed system
as a revealed life
he will fold up,
quiet as the heliotrope
after sunset closes its arms,
quiet as the desert
after the nomads have left.

This is a story that admits of no essence larger than
    the human.
This is a story that sees only the solar system,
    although the whole galaxy is known to be extant.

A girl grows up
pinning her every heart's beat
on her father,   her mother the enemy
always exacting requirements of good behavior
from her.

As she gets older she sees parts of herself
are her mother, she studies with fear of failure in college
is alone with fear that she will do wrong
& cannot rip her mother from the parts of her body
she hates, but wants to love.

                    She begins to fall "in love"
with men who desire
her crystalline body,
her ability to build them up
and make them feel powerful,
her laughter and gaiety and lack of selfishness.

The main thing she has learned so far
is how to make others happy,
a spirit of generosity that allows her
to talk better about another's troubles
than her own.

She confuses her own worth
                                    with the love they give her.
One after another she adores,
worships, they seem so brilliant
and so much a part of the world

They love her because
she pleases them
goes away when she should
and makes them feel good.

                    Finally she dimly perceives
                    that this, her life
                    has been a pattern of seeming rights
                    & wrongs only obvious to herself

                    when she tries to explain it to her mother
                    & her sisters
                    they suggest that she get out of the expensive college
                    & transfer to the State University close to home

if she is really that ungrateful

She spins into a whole other love affair
this time with a man who is married
who is much older than she
& who in time begins to seem corrupt
He comes down hard on closet fags in the government
the ad agency which seemed glamorous from Denver
now that he is in New York, seems shabby
& he with his cigar and new clothes
seems sad and middle-class

She runs and runs and runs in a stark terror
& marries a man she has loved,
has kept communicating with through other love affairs.
Sometimes she doesn't wildly desire him
as she has these other men
whom she has responded to out of need & passion

She learns a whole new life
her worth apart from her sexuality
is very important for the first time;
she works hard, reading, learning, writing
until again
            each day
she begins to feel she is running hard,
out of breath,
                trying to be bright enough

to read enough
to write enough
to not be emotional but articulate,
            logical and conceptual

She has to fight for survival
    in a world where she's hardly learned the terms
    and yearns to make her world *just hers*
    where she will have to live up to
            nothing

                    what is obscure is whether the world
                        she inhabits is really like this
                    or whether she exacts this pressure
                        from herself

They go around the country
live in different places
make a family   believe in ideals
peace and contentment
and help one another when each is down

Most of the time
            what they have is to her
a noble experiment
            she totally believes in

but sometimes the whole horror
                    of her early years comes back
(as it does for him too

& she feels stupid
                    & only desirous of a paternal affection
of a man she can please who will
                    take care of her, shield her
from all she is scared of

She rejects her husband in her mind
in these moments
as everything she must live up to
she feels incapable of ever pleasing him or
            herself and begins to slide downhill,
confusing mother and husband and lovers and father

                    Because life goes on, & people strain
to keep track of the events
she meets a man
who after seven years of marriage is the first
entity to excite her admiration & imagination
He is resident in their world
& brings out in her
all her earlier reactions towards a type of mind
            she admired and desired in a steady pattern, for years

He is either the great force in her life,
the great love
or a neurotic distraction from solving these problems.

The great question to her is an ultimate one
& yet one that whisks away when stars,
hurricanes, natural forces are mentioned:

whether there *are* great loves
or whether humans when they mature
stop such thinking
                & concentrate on their business,
on making a satisfactory life for all members of the family
on spiritual awareness and the growth of consciousness
given how difficult life is
for everyone,
                becoming aware of their confusions
and working to improve them
& making each other happier

Believing in family
she conceives a second child
although her husband is unsure it's wise

        This is seen by the new man
        (however flippantly said) as armor

to protect herself from finding the aggression
to be with him.

The months which follow
are a difficult time
when she is physiologically sick
she is confused psychologically
& yet as the pregnancy progresses she finds
the new child
reason enough
to be clear on these things
so pursues them
as others pursue endangered species

When she is most embattled
against the various parts of herself
most faint
in the outline she casts against her world
the man becomes all-important & seems to be
        a shadow of the only self
        she has really known   the old self
        of childhood & narcissism which was "unselfish"

She talks to him in the old way
        endlessly leads him out
        so he is telling her his whole life
        she wants to set an elaborate trap for him
        & he feels chased, but since he is lonely

he rather likes it, as of course it flatters his ego

When she is with him
for long periods of time (never alone,
        never able to really act anything out)
she tires of him,
or they tire of the societal talk
they must do   people grow tired & just want to
go to bed   or go away from each other

When she has not seen him
for a long time it is hardest
the shadow builds in strength & visage
so by the time she does see him,
it is too charged, she is too intense
Her own powers against this force
seem to wane
                & she is heavily weighted down,
                sullen & depressed & obnoxious,
because she is lusting after a life
she has known only as child
which is gone

Again and again she falls into these vistas
& is pulled out by the least
        intellectual concentration
        on any one thing
So gradually she develops a motivation

to learn about all there is
in the world
stronger and more hungry than any reason
          she had as a college girl or a child
As she learns she finds relief
          in the constructions of thought
          in mastering difficult material
The matrices
     take the pressure off her
to decide who she loves
          who she is attracted to
          whether she is attractive to X
          whether she feels responsive to her husband

She learns how to survive
          in this new way
& begins to value the connections
she can make
between these different ways of
   perceiving phenomena

She comes to see she is One
          who can watch inside & outside with equal
                    insight & pleasure

She begins to feel worthwhile
& churns out great batches of material
based on her present & past knowledge

111

She is capable of participating
        in the world & takes part in it
        more and more

Still, every day
she fights
to keep the balance
that is so hard to maintain between
these early horrors, the regressions
        & her present growth

            The sun shines
            wind blows unseasonably warm in December
            the comet is coming & they worry about California
            yet inside, with the growing child coming along,
            she finds peacefulness
            from having worked through
                a certain amount of this

Is it called Barre Hill Road?

That incredible arch down
from which you look

see the whole town laid out
flat in your palm

incredible
it takes your breath away

What is it about

Vermont towns
from above!

That you are always wanting to
climb the surrounding hills

Because you know
what it'll look like

The town

the mist as far as you can see
the whole valley, laid out

smooth
as your upturned palm

O
little creature-culture
O,
little animal garden
can you make the transition
from our village house
where we are whirring around in
a vortex of boundaries & ideas
to her animal rolling hills
where everything sprawls & bawls
& you are piling over hill & dale?

O little mohawk
you probably have it in hand
better than I
but there's a seer here
who's given me three words
I hoe by:
    tender
    self-absolving
    rutabagas.

Sheathed like a slim foot
in this special beautiful shoe of
on the brink, the necessity of being always
able to produce good work
making in me a taut tension so that

the lassitudes other men & women
allow themselves are no longer possible,
condition of being always about to explode

into a thousand slivers of glass
or an honest man's hand

steam rising billowing clouds
from Vermont Yankee, her 90 cows
graze, their milk laced with radioactivity
of which she does not have clear *proof*
"I have to admit it's kind of pretty,"
she says, "on a hazy day the steam billowing
up in those clouds across the river . . ."

O river of waters cooling evil
To be so far from that as to swim
underwater in a river of madness so the

            very abstraction the life,
            the work plays with promotes
            this quality of sure hits,
            a pressure to not miss very often,
            so the next action unimportant unless
            laced with risk & possibility of destruction

Still I have stayed alive
these thirty years, & so
has he & he

O dont you think
we should spend a long time together
         I sd, knowing I cd go off the road,
         children in the car, any moment &
         increasing my chances by seeking him out;
         no time is propitious for the end of the world

I can see now how people entwine
              themselves in calamitous events,
Malgré their intentions,
their sense of orderliness;

It is one thing to play tennis
aggressively in the morning sunlight
the ball touching splintered keystones of inquiry
            another to say, I will come
            & carry you off someday

                        * * *

                  We can't make it anymore
in an orderly fashion,
the ideas cloud the waves coming in,
sands absorb a cycle of the same water

                        Lawrence pacing the porch of his
                        beachfront cottage outside Sydney
                        writing *Kangaroo*, sun in the waves
                        wondering what man is coming to,
                        what he himself should be doing,
                        working every morning,
                        working every morning.